Captain Innocencio

(Rex Beach)

The moon was not yet two hours high when Captain Innocencio prepared to let himself over the side of the schooner. Outside, the Caribbean was all agleam, save where the coral reef teeth gnashed it into foam; inside, a sand beach, yellow in the moonlight, curved east and west like a causeway until the distance swallowed it. Back of that lay the groves of cocoanut trees, their plumes waving in the undying undulations that had never ceased since first the trade-winds breathed upon them. Beneath the palms themselves the jungle was ink-black, patched here and there with silver. The air was heavy with the slow rumble of an ever restless surf, and, all about, the sea was whispering, whispering, as if minded to tell its mysteries.

It was the sort of night that had ever wakened wild impulses in Captain Innocencio's breast. It was on such a night that he had first felt the touch of a woman's lips; it was on such another night that he had first felt a man's warm blood upon his hands. That had been long ago, to be sure, in far Haiti, and since that time both of those sensations had lost much of their novelty, for he had lived fast and hard and his exile had plunged him into many evils. It was on such a moonlight night, also, that he had begun his wanderings, fleeing southward between moonrise and moonset, southward, whither all the scum of the Indies floated. But, even to this day, when it came to the full of a February moon, with the fragrant salt trades blowing and the sound of a throbbing surf beneath it, the sated, stagnant blood of Captain Innocencio went hot, his thin mulatto face grew hard, and a certain strange exultance blazed within him.

His crew had long since come to recognize this frenzy, and had they now beheld him, poised half nude at the rail, his fierce eyes bent upon the forbidden shore, they would have ventured no remark. As it happened, however, they were all asleep, all three of them, and the Captain's lips curled scornfully. What could black men know about such subtleties as the call of moonlight? What odds to them if yonder palm fronds beckoned? They had no curiosity, no resentfulness; otherwise they, too, might have dared to break the San Blas law.

It was four years now since he had first begun to sail this coast, and even though he was known on every *cay* and bay from Nombre de Dios to Tiburon, and even though it was recognized that the Señor "Beel Weelliams" paid proper price for cocoa- and ivory-nuts, his head trader had never beaten down the people's distrust. On the contrary, their vigilance had increased, if anything, and now, after four years of scrupulous fair dealing, he, Captain Innocencio, was still compelled to sleep off-shore and under guard, like any common stranger.

It had made the Haitian laugh, at first; for who would wish to harm a San Blas woman, with the streets of Colon but a hundred miles to the west? Then, as the months crept into years, and for voyage after voyage he never saw a San Blas woman's face, he became furious. Next he grew angry, then sullen, and a sense of injury burned into him. He set his wits against theirs; but invariably the sight of his schooner's sails was a signal for the women to melt away--invariably, when night came, and he and his blacks had been herded back aboard their craft, the women returned, and the sound of their voices served to fan the flame within his breast.

Night after night, in sheltered coves or open river-mouths, the Captain of the *Espirita* had lain, belly down, upon the little roof of the deckhouse, his head raised serpent-wise, his gloomy eyes fixed upon the cook-fires in the distance.

And when some woman's figure suddenly stood out against the fire-lit walls, or when some maiden's song came floating seaward, he had breathed curses in his bastard French, and directed a message of hate at the sentinel he knew was posted in the jungle shadows. At times he had railed at his crew of spiritless Jamaican "niggers," and lusted for a following of his own kind--men with the French blood of his island in their veins, men who would follow where the moonlight flickered. He had even gone so far, at one time, as to search the water-fronts from Port Limon to Santa Marta in quest of such fellows; he had winnowed the offscourings of the four seas gathered there, but without success. They were villainous chaps, for the main part, crossed with many creeds and colors, and ready for any desperate venture; but he could not find three helpers of sufficient hardihood to tamper with the San Blas virgins. Instead, they had retold him the tales he already knew by heart: tales of swift and sudden retribution overtaking blacks and whites; retribution that did not halt even at the French or the hated *Americanos*. They told him that, of all the motley races gathered here since earliest Spanish days, the San Blas blood alone retained its purity. It was his boss, the Señor Williams, who had gone back farthest into history, and it was he likewise who had threatened him with prompt discharge if he presumed to trespass. The Señor Williams was not one to permit profitable trade relations to be jeopardized by the whim of a Haitian mulatto.

Innocencio had listened passively, then, when alone, smiled. He owed no loyalty. He had no law. Even the name he went by was a fiction.

He continued to make his trips, and when he came driving in ahead of the humming trade-winds, his schooner laden with the treasures of the islands, the back streets of Colon awoke to his presence and prepared to greet him. But, however loud the music in the *cantinas,* however fierce the exultation of the liquor in him, however wild the orgy into which he plunged, he could never quite drown the memory of those sleepless vigils far to the eastward; and ever in his quiet moments he heard the faint song of San Blas women wafted by the breath of the sea, ever in his dreams he saw the slim outlines of girlish figures, black against a flaring camp-fire.

Four years this thing had grown upon him, during which he haunted the San Blas coast. And then, one night, he slipped over side and swam ashore. It was not so dangerous as it seemed, for, once he had gained the shelter of the jungle, no less than a pack of hounds could have followed him, inasmuch as the thickets were laced by a network of trails that gave forth no sound to naked soles, and the rustling branches overhead, played upon by the never-ceasing breeze, drowned all signal of his presence. Once he had defied the tribal law, he knew no further peace. It was like the first taste of blood to an animal. Thereafter Innocencio the outlaw, whose name was a symbol of daring, became a jackal prowling through the midnight glades, casting the scent of the villages, and staring with hungry eyes from just beyond the shadow's edge. Rather, he became a panther, for in his caution was no cowardice, only a feline patience. Village after village he hunted until he had marked his prey. Then he waited to spring.

To be sure, he had never spoken with the girl, nor even seen her clearly; but the sound of her voice made him tremble.

To accomplish even this much had taken many trips of the *Espirita,* had meant many sleepless nights and some few tense moments when only the shadows saved him from betrayal. There had been times, for instance, when the quick simulation of a wild pig's grunt or the purr of *el tigre* had served to explain the sound of his retreat; other times when he had stood motionless in the shadows, the evil, rust-red blade of his machete matching the hue of his half-nude body.

To-night he crouched behind the deckhouse and ran his eye over the schooner in one final glance of caution. It was well that all should be in readiness, for the moment of his spring might come within the hour, or, if not to-night, then to-morrow night, a week, a month, a year from to-night, and then a tackle fouled or a block jammed might spell destruction.

He thrust his head through a loop of the leathern scabbard, and swung the huge knife back until it lay along the crease between his shoulders; then he seized the port stay and let himself softly downward over side. The water rose to his chin. Without a ripple, he glided into the moonlight astern, and a moment later his round black head was no more than a piece of bobbing drift borne landward by the current.

Down past the village he swam, noting the rows of dugouts on the beach. He saw a blot in the big mahogany *cayuca,* a great canoe hewn from one priceless trunk, and recognized it for the sentinel. On he floated, then worked his way ashore behind the little point. Once he felt the hard, smooth sand beneath his soles, he waited until a cloud obscured the moon, and, when the light broke through again, he was dripping underneath a wide-leaved breadfruit tree at the jungle's edge. Removing the machete from his neck, he wrung the water from his cotton trousers. Over his head a night-bird croaked hoarsely.

The girl was at her father's house, tending a fire on the dirt floor. It was a large house, for the old man was rich in daughters, and, by the San Blas rule, their husbands had come to live with him. He had waxed fat long ago on their labors, and now only this youngest one remained unmarried. But the ceremony was set. Innocencio had heard the news upon his arrival three days before, and had grudgingly bought a big store of tortoise-shell from the groom-to-be, knowing full well that the money was intended for the wedding celebration. Markeeña was the fellow's name, a straight, upstanding youth who more than once had excited the Haitian's admiration for his skill with a canoe. But since that day the latter had regarded him with smoldering eyes.

The big thatched roof with its bark-floored loft stood on posts blackened by the smoke of many feasts; there were no walls. The jungle crept close to it from the rear, and hence the watcher could witness every movement of the girl as she passed between the hammocks or stooped to her task. He could see, for instance, the play of her dark round shoulders above the neck of her shift. He ground his yellow teeth and gripped the moist earth with the soles of his naked feet, as a tiger bares its claws before the leap.

It was very hard to wait.

For an hour he stood there. Once a dog came to him and sniffed, then, recognizing a frequent visitor, returned to the house and resumed its slumber beside the fire. From the houses beyond came the sound of voices, of a child crying querulously, and of a woman quieting it. People came and went. An old hag began pounding grain in a mortar, crooning in a broken voice. The girl's father came rolling into view, and. after a word to her, struggled heavily up the ladder to his bed. He was snoring almost before the structure had ceased to creak beneath him. In the thicket a multitude of nocturnal sounds arose, the insect chorus of the night.

And then, before Innocencio realized what she was up to, the girl had stolen swiftly out and past him, so close that he could hear the scuff of her sandals on the beaten path. The next instant he had glided from cover and fallen in behind, his pulses leaping, his long, lithe muscles rippling; but he moved as silently as a shadow.

Had he been a less accomplished bushman he might have lost her, for she plunged into the jungle unhesitatingly. However, he had long ago learned these trails by daylight, and knew them better than the lines of his own palm; hence every moonlit turn, every flash of her white slip, found him close upon her track.

It puzzled him at first to discover her reason for this unexpected sally, but soon he decided she must be bent upon some mission. Then, when he saw that she purposely avoided the village and was bending toward the open palm grove abreast of his anchorage, he knew she must be going to a tryst. So Markeeña was the sentinel! That fellow in the mahogany *cayuca* was her lover! Innocencio, the dissolute, felt a flame of rage suffuse him; and when, at last, his quarry emerged into the mysterious half-light under the high roof of palms, and paused, he strode after her. She gave the melancholy call of the night-bird that had sounded in the breadfruit tree over his head earlier in the evening; then, seeing him close beside her, uttered a little cry of pleasure. Not until he was too near for flight did she discover her mistake, and then she seemed to freeze. Her utter silence was more menacing than a scream.

It was the instant for which he had schooled himself, so he spoke to her in her own tongue:

"Make no outcry! I will not harm you."

She drew back, at which he laid his great, bony hand upon her, his eyes blazing. She was deathly frightened, being little more than a child.

"I have waited for you many nights," he explained. "I feared you would never come." Then, as she continued to stare up at him uncomprehendingly, he ran on: "I am Innocencio, the trader. Every night I have watched you at your work. I want you for my woman."

Her voice had forsaken her utterly, but she struggled weakly, so he tightened his grip until his fingers sank into her flesh. She began to gasp as if from a swift run; the open neck of her garment slipped down over one shoulder; her eyes were distended until he saw them ringed about with white. The terror of this tall yellow man with the hungry eyes robbed her of power, and she let him drag her toward the lapping water as if she were no more than some weak, wild thing that he had trapped.

Of course she knew him, for, while the San Blas law may banish women, it can not blind them, and she too had studied him from concealment. Although his words had made no impression whatever upon her, his grasp and the direction he was drawing her in at last translated what was in his mind. Then she burst into life. But she made no outcry, for it takes strength to scream, and every atom of her force was directed against his. She began to moan. Her every muscle writhed. With her free hand she tore at his entwining fingers, but they were like jungle creepers that no human strength could serve to loosen. And all the time he drew her with him, speaking softly.

Then she felt him pause, and her distracted vision beheld

another figure entering the shadows from the shore. She called to her lover hoarsely, and saw him halt at the strange note, peering inward for a sight of her. She voiced words now for the first time, crying:

"The stranger! The stranger!"

Then, hearing the scrape of her captor's machete as he drew it from its scabbard, she renewed her struggle more fiercely.

Captain Innocencio held the girl at his left side until the last moment, balancing the great knife-blade as if to try his arm; then, when the Indian was close upon him, coming straight as a dart, he freed himself. A slanting moonbeam showed Markeeña's ferocious visage and his upraised weapon, but the Haitian met the falling blow with a fierce upward stroke that once before had done him service. It was the stroke that had made him an exile years before.

Innocencio's physical strength had ever been his pride, if also his undoing; above all things, he prided himself upon the dexterity and vigor of his wrist. His early training on that blood-red Caribbean isle, and a later life in thicket and swamp, had served to transform the cumbrous weapon into a thing of life at his hands. More than once, for instance, he had harried a serpent until it struck, for the mere satisfaction of severing its head in midcourse; and now he felt the wide blade enter flesh. Before his antagonist could cry out twice he had slashed again, this time downward as if to split a green cocoanut. The next instant he had seized the girl as she fled into the jungle.

But she had found her voice at last, and he was forced to muffle her with his palm. When they were out into the moonlight, however, with the dry sand up to their ankles, he let her breathe; then, pointing with his machete to the *Espirita* lying white and ghostlike in the offing, he drove her down into the warm sea until it reached her waist.

"Swim!" he ordered, and, when she would have renewed the alarm, he raised his blade, grimly threatening to call the sharks with her blood.

"Swim!" he repeated, and she struck out, with him at her shoulder.

But the village was roused. A confused clamor betrayed its bewilderment, and, before the swimmers had won more than half way to the schooner, figures came running along the shore. Innocencio cautioned the girl to hold her tongue, and she obeyed him, thoroughly cowed by his roughness. She turned upon her side and swam with her face close to his, her eyes fixed upon him curiously, wonderingly. Her easy progress through the water showed that her fright had largely vanished, and showed likewise that had the Haitian been no uncommon swimmer himself she might have distanced him. All the way out to the boat she stared at him with that same fixed look, maintaining her position at his side. The moon and the salt brine in his eyes played him tricks, else he might have fancied her to be half smiling, as if in some strange exaltation akin to his own.

Not until he finally dragged her, panting, to the deck of the *Espirita,* and her white-clad figure stood out clearly from the shore, did her tribesmen realize the nature of the alarm. Then the vibrant turmoil suddenly stilled for the space of a full minute, while the enormity of the outrage made itself felt. They drew together at the edge of the sea, staring open-mouthed, amazed, before they raised their blood-cry.

The man and woman rested a moment, their eyes upon the

shore, and where they stood twin pools of water blackened the deck. Then Innocencio turned to look upon his prey. The girl's flimsy cotton shift was molded to her figure, and he saw that she was even fairer than he had pictured; so, in spite of his need for haste, he paused to gloat upon the favor the moon and the salt sea had rendered him. As for her, she flung his glance back bravely until he wrenched open the cabin hatch and pointed to the dark interior. Then she weakened. But she had a will of her own, it seemed, for she refused to be locked inside. He strode toward her, and she clutched the rigging desperately, turning her glance to one of appeal.

"You may come up in a moment," he translated, but still she clung to the stay. "If you try to escape--" He scowled upon her terribly, at which she shook her head. Having already tasted her strength, he knew there was no time to force her, so he leaped at his crew. The three blacks were snoring forward of the deckhouse, so he seized a bucket of water at the rail and sluiced them into wakefulness, keeping his eye upon the girl meanwhile. When he saw that in truth she made no move, he let his caution slip, and raged over the ship like a tiger, beating his half-clad crew ahead of him with the flat of his machete; but by the time they had gained their wits the tribesmen were massing at the canoes. As the mainsail rose creaking he broke out the jib with his own hand, then with one stroke of his knife severed the manila mooring-rope, and the *Espirita* fell off slowly ahead' of the breeze. Innocencio ran back to spur his befuddled "niggers" to further activity, only to find the girl still motionless, her eyes following his every movement. Under his curses, the schooner slowly raised her wings and the night wind began to strain at the cordage.

But at last, when the Jamaicans were fully awake to the state of affairs, they threatened mutiny, whereat the mulatto flung himself upon them so savagely that they scattered to arm themselves with whatever weapons lay at hand. Then they huddled amidship, rolling their eyes and praying; for out from the shore came a long mahogany *cayuca,* and it was full of straight-haired men.

It takes a sailing-craft some time to gain its momentum, and as yet the full strength of the trades had not struck the *Espirita;* hence the canoe overtook her rapidly. Innocencio called to one of his men and gave him the tiller, then took stand beside the girl, the naked blade of his weapon once more beneath his arm.

The schooner's helmsman gave himself to God, while the cordage overhead began to whine as the deck rose. It was upon the Haitian's lips to warn his pursuers off, when one of them called to the girl, bidding her leap. Innocencio heard the breath catch in her throat, but she made no move, and the command was repeated.

This time she answered by some exclamation that he did not understand, whereat the canoe-men ceased paddling, as if her word had paralyzed them. They hurled their voices at her savagely, but she remained motionless, the while the waters beneath her began to foam and bubble. The *Espirita's* crew ceased their prayers, and in the silence that ensued the sea whispered at the bow as the craft listed more heavily under the full force of the wind.

Innocencio could not fathom the meaning of the subdued colloquy among the San Blas men, so he shouted a warning, but, strangely enough, they made no answer. They only crouched, with paddles motionless, staring at the dimming figures facing them, until the *Espirita,* "wing and wing" ahead of the trades, was no larger than a sea-gull. As yet they had not learned of the other tragedy hidden in the shadow of the palms; had they suspected what lay weltering at the edge of a trampled moonlit glade behind them, no threat of Innocencio's, no plea of his new-found woman, could have held them back.

Once the schooner was under way, the Haitian led the girl to the deckhouse and thrust her roughly inside, closing the hatch. Then with his own hands he took his craft through the reef and out into the leaping Caribbean. Not until the San Blas coast was a mere charcoal line upon the port quarter and the salt spray was driving high did he deliver over the helm; but at last he gave his crew instructions for the night, and went below, closing and bolting the hatch behind him. When the smoky lamp that swung between the bunks was lit and its yellow gleam had illumined the interior, he saw the girl's eyes fast upon him. He went toward her across the tilting floor, and she arose to meet him, smiling.

II

Señor Bill Williams was in a fine rage.

"Didn't you like your job?" he questioned. Innocencio shrugged languidly.

"Oh, yes! The job was good."

"You knew I'd fire you!"

"Si!"

The American tempered his indignant glare with a hint of curiosity. "You must love that San Blas girl."

"What do you say?"

"You must love her--better than your job, at least?"

"Si, señor! I suppose so."

"What is she like, Innocencio?"

"Well, she is just like other women. All women are alike-- only some are fat. One time I had a female from Martinique, and she acted just the same as this one."

"Humph! If she is like all the others, what the devil made you--do it?"

"Señor, you have plenty of money, and yet one night I saw you bet two thousand pesos on the *rouge.* Why did you do that, eh?"

"That is altogether different."

The Haitian smiled. "I am tired of these females at Colon. They are common people--very common. Then, too, those San Blas people, they are so scared that somebody is going to steal a woman! Maybe if they had left me sleep on shore I would never have noticed no woman at all. But they don't trust me, so, sure enough--I steal one."

"And you say she came willingly?" queried Williams incredulously.

"Oh, yes! When her people commanded her to jump from my schooner, she refused them. I did not understand at the time, but by an' by she told me." He swelled his chest with pride. "I guess she never seen so brave a man as me before. Eh, señor?"

"Humph! I guess I never will *sabe* you niggers," acknowledged the American.

Innocencio corrected his recent employer, but without show of the slightest heat:

"I am no nigger, señor; I am Haitian. She is San Blas Indian. My father was not even so dark as me. Black men have thick heads and you have to beat them, but nobody ever beat me, not even a white man. When those niggers sleep I lie awake and study; I make schemes. That is why I left Haiti."

"Do you understand that you've got me into a hell of a fix? I've got to take a trip down there myself to square things."

Innocencio lighted a black cigarette and blew the smoke

through his nose. Evidently other people's troubles did not concern him. Recognizing the futility of reproach or indignation, the former speaker continued:

"But see here, now! This girl? You can't keep her."

"Eh? Who's going to take her away?" interrogated the Haitian quickly. "Bah! One man tried that, and--I killed him with my machete." His thin lips drew back at the memory, and for an instant his yellow face showed a hint of what had made his reputation.

"She won't stay with you."

"Oh, yes, she will. She was wild, very wild at first, but--she will stay."

"And how about her people? They're bad *hombres*. Even the government lets them alone--fortunately for you."

"They won't make no trouble about that Markeeña. He is quite dead, I think."

"By Jove! You're a cold-blooded brute."

"Señor! You told me once that nobody had ever married a San Blas female, eh?"

"Yes. Even the old Spaniards tried it, but the blood is clean, so far; something unusual, too, in this country."

Innocencio began to laugh silently, as if at a joke.

"Some day, maybe, you will see a San Blas half-breed playing in the streets of Colon," said he.

"I don't believe it."

"I'll bet you my wages--two hundred pesos. Come! I'll show you."

"You get out of here," said the American roughly. "That's something I don't allow anybody to joke about." And, when the mulatto had gone, he continued aloud: "By Heaven, this is sure a tough country for a white man!"

Innocencio strode through the streets toward the swamp that lies behind the town, oblivious to the grilling midday heat that smote him from above, from the concrete walks beneath, and from the naked walls on every side. It was before the days of the American occupation, and the streets were nothing more than open cesspools, the stench from which offended sorely. Buzzards flapped among the naked children at play in the mire beside the sewer-ditches.

The place was filled with everything unhealthy, and had long been known as the earth's great festering sore. Neither the Orient nor the farthest tropics boasted another spot like Colon, or Aspinwall, as it had been called, with its steaming, hip-deep streets and its brilliant flowering grave-yards. So hateful had it proved, in fact, that when seamen signed articles binding themselves to work their ships into any corner of the globe, they inserted a clause exempting them from entering Aspinwall.

Now, however, the town was lively, for this was the dry season, when the fever was at its lowest, and the resorts were filled with the flotsam and jetsam of a tropic world. It was a polyglot town, moreover, set upon a fever-ridden mangrove isle serving as one terminus of the world's short cut, and in it had collected all the parasites that live upon the moving herd.

The French work of digging had but served to augment the natural population by a no less desperate set from overseas, and now from the open doors of their cubby-holes women of every color greeted the passer-by.

Innocencio, whose last exploit was already a thing of gossip, received unusual attention, there being no color line in Colon town. White, yellow, and black women fawned upon him and bade him tarry; but he merely paused to listen or to fan their admiration by a word, then idled onward, pleased at the notice he evoked.

Once fairly out of the pest-hole, he threaded his way through the swamp toward the other shore of the island. Blue land-crabs scuttled among the mangrove roots at his approach; the place was noisy with the hum of insects; on every hand the heated mud gave forth a sound like the smack of huge moist lips. But on the other side he came into a different domain. Here the sea breeze banished the hovering miasma, the shore was of powdered coral sand, a litter of huts drowsed beneath a grove of cocoa palms, while a fleet of *cayucas* lay moored to stakes inside the breakers or bleaching in the sun.

Captain Innocencio was a person of some importance here, for, besides his occupation as a trader, he exacted toll from a score or more of lazy blacks. They were a lawless crew, gathered from the remotest corners of the Indies, and composed of Jamaicans, "Bajans," and Saint Lucians, all reared to easy life and ripe for such an occasional crafty pilgrimage as Innocencio might devise. They had gathered around him naturally, paying him scant revenue, to be sure, yet offering a certain loyalty that had uses. Although the village was but a mile from the town itself, Innocencio's word was law; and when the Colombian soldiers were called upon to visit the spot, they came in numbers, never singly.

The girl was seated on the rickety porch of his cabin, her feet drawn under her, her chin upon her knees. The other women were gossiping loudly, staring at her from a distance; but her black eyes only smoldered sullenly. He swore at the curious negro wenches, and sent the girl about her household duties, then stretched himself in the shade and eyed her complacently until he fell asleep.

It was a week later that one of his men came to him breathlessly to announce that the San Blas Indians were in the town.

"How many?" queried Innocencio.

"Four boat-loads."

"Did they come to trade?"

"Oh, yes, boss."

This was no unusual thing, for they often displayed their little cargoes of nuts and fruits and vegetables upon the water-front. Innocencio rose lazily and stretched, then, calling the woman, explained the tidings to her.

"I will go see them," he announced finally.

"Oh, boss," cried the black man, "they will kill you!"

He shrugged his brawny shoulders, and, thrusting the machete beneath his arm, took the trail out through the mangrove swamp.

Straight to the Colon water-front he went, and there flaunted himself before the men from down the coast. Here and there he strolled, casting back their looks of hatred with a bravado that attracted all the idlers in the neighborhood. Wenches nudged each other and tittered nervously, pointing him out and telling anew the story of his daring. Men watched him with wondering admiration, and he heard them murmuring:

"Ah, that Innocencio!"

"El diablo!"

"And so brave! He would fight an army."

"See the great arms of him, and the eye like a tiger."

It was the keenest pleasure he had ever tasted.

But as for his enemies, they kept their silence. They bartered their stock, and, having made their purchases, raised sail and scudded away down the coast whence they had come.

Innocencio got drunk that night--for who could withstand the lavish flattery that poured from every *cantina* up and down the length of Bottle Alley? Who could resist the smiles of the chalk-faced females of Cash Street, all eager to laud his bravery? Sometime before morning he reeled into his shack beneath the palms, to find the woman waiting fearfully. He cursed at her for staring at him so, and fell upon his bed.

In the months that followed he seldom lost an opportunity of showing himself to the San Blas men when they came to town; but in time this pleasure palled as all others had, for his woman's kindred seemed incapable of resentment. Gradually, also, he became accustomed to her presence, and spent much of his time among the women of the Cash Street dives. On one occasion he returned from an orgy of this sort to find her talking to one of his men, a young Barbadian with a giant's frame. It was only by accident, due to the liquor in him, that his hand went wild and he missed killing the fellow; then he beat the woman unmercifully.

Chancing to meet the Señor Williams on the street some time later, he said:

"*Buenas dias, señor!* You see, Captain Innocencio is still alive and the woman has not run away."

His former employer grunted, as if neither phenomenon were worthy of comment.

"I've heard how you rub it into those San Blas fellows," Williams remarked. "I can't understand why they never avenged Markeeña."

"Bah! They have heard of me," said the Haitian boastfully; then, with a grin, "You remember our bet, señor?"

"I never made you a bet," the American denied hotly. "But I've a mind to. I've been here ten years, and I think I know those people."

"Two hundred pesos!"

"You'll never have a child by her. They won't allow it. They'll get her, and you too, in ample time. I tell you, their blood is clean."

"Two hundred pesos that she brings me a San Blas half-breed within two months," smiled the mulatto insolently.

And Williams exclaimed: "I'll do it. It's worth two hundred 'silver' to see a miracle."

"*Bueno!* I'll bring him to you when he comes."

Thereafter Innocencio gave over beating the woman.

Back at the little settlement beyond the swamp the coming event did not pass without comment, and although the black women were kind to their straight-haired neighbor, she never made friends with them, nor did she ever accompany Innocencio to town. On the contrary, she seemed obsessed by an ever-present dread, and whenever she heard that her own people were near she concealed herself and did not appear again until they were gone. Bred into her deepest conscience was the certainty that her tribe would make a desperate attempt to preserve its most sacred tradition, and hence, as the days dragged on and her condition became more pronounced, her fears increased likewise. She began to look forward to the birth of the child as the crisis upon which her own life hinged. Innocencio did his best to dissipate her fears, explaining boastfully that the mere mention of his name was ample protection for her, and, did he wish it, not even the army of the Republic could take her from him. But still she would not be convinced.

And then, in the dark of the December moon, the expected came. It was the season when the rains were at their heaviest, when rust and rot might be felt by the fingers. A gray mold had crept over all things indoors; a myriad of insect pests burdened the air. In the rare intervals between showers every faintest draft deluged the huts from the dripping palm leaves overhead. From the swamp arose a noxious vapor whenever the sun exposed itself; the tree-toads shrilled incessantly. Outside, the surf maintained its sullen murmur, and through the gloom of starless nights its phosphorescent outlines rushed across the reef like phantom serpents in parade.

In the dead of a night like this the visitors arrived.

Even the heavy animal slumber of the blacks was broken by the scream that issued from the hut of Captain Innocencio. And then the sound of such fighting! The negroes might have rushed to the assistance of their leader had it not been for the echo of that awful woman-cry hovering over the village like a shadow. It filled the air and hung there, saturating the breathless night with such unnamable terror that the wakened children began to whimper and the women buried their heads in the ragged bedding to keep it out. Death was among them, and the bravest cowered, while through the quivering silence came the sounds of a mighty combat, lasting for such an interminable time that the listeners became hysterical.

At length they discovered that the night was dead again, save for the sudden patter of raindrops on the thatches when the palm fronds stirred. One of them called shrilly, and another answered, but they did not venture forth. Afterward they fancied they had heard the thrust of paddles in the lagoon and strange voices dwindling away to seaward, but they were not sure. Eventually, however, the stillness got upon them more fearfully than the former noises had, and they stirred. Then, in time, they heard the voice of Innocencio himself cursing faintly, as if from a great distance. A light showed through the cracks of a hut, and Nicholas, the least timid, emerged with a lantern held on high. He summoned the rest around him, then went toward the black shadow of Innocencio's dwelling with a score of white-eyed, dusky faces at his shoulder.

The door was down, and from the threshold they could see what the front room contained. It was Nicholas who, with chattering teeth and nerveless fingers, dragged a blanket from the bed and covered the woman's figure. It was he who traced the feeble voice to the wreck of a room behind, and strove to lift Innocencio out of the welter in which he lay. But the Haitian blasted him with curses for opening his wounds; so they propped him against the wall by his direction, and bound him about with strips torn from the mattress. Then he called for a cigarette, and its ashes were upon his breast when the French doctor arrived from the hospital on the Point.

When the white man's work was done, the mulatto addressed him weakly:

"Will m'sieu' do me a great favor?"

"Certainly."

"M'sieu' is acquainted with the American, Señor Williams?"

"Oui."

"Will *m'sieu' le docteur* please to tell him that Captain Innocencio has won his wager."

"I don't understand."

"Listen! In the room yonder, under the bed, m'sieu' will find a little boy baby rolled up in a blanket. The woman heard them at the door, and she was just in time. Oh, she knew they would be coming."

The French doctor nodded his comprehension.

"But--your wife herself?" said he. "Perhaps when you are well again you can have your vengeance. The soldiers will--"

"Bah! What is the use?" interrupted Innocencio. "The world is full of women." Then, strangely enough, he bared his yellow teeth in a smile of rarest tenderness. "But this boy of mine! They came to kill him, m'sieu', and to show that the San Blas blood can not be crossed; but the woman was too quick of wit. They did not find him, praise God! *Le docteur* has seen many children, perhaps, but never a child like this." He ran on with a father's tender boastfulness. "M'sieu' will note the back and the legs of him. And, see, he did not even cry, the little man! Oh! he is like his father for bravery. He will be my vengeance, for he has the San Blas blood in him; and he will be a man like me, too. Bring him to me quickly; I must see him again." He was still babbling fondly to the negroes about him when the doctor reappeared, empty-handed.

"The child is dead," said the white man simply, and in the silence Innocencio rose to a sitting posture. His fierce eyes grew wild with a fright that had never been there until this moment; and then, before they could prevent him, he had gained his feet. He waved them aside and went into the room of death, walking like a strong man. A candle guttering beside the open window betrayed the utter nakedness of the place. With one movement of his great, bony hands he ripped the planks of the bed asunder and stared downward. Then he turned to the east and, raising his arms above his head, gave a terrible cry. He began to sway, and even as the doctor leaped save him he fell with a crash.

It was Nicholas who told the priest that the French doctor would not let them move him; for he lay upon his face at the feet of the San Blas woman, his arms flung outward like the arms of a cross.

THE END

www.ingramcontent.com/pod-product-compliance
Lightning Source LLC
Chambersburg PA
CBHW060352290526
45791CB00004B/1643